STORMS AND SNOW, SKIS AND SOX!

New England's Weather Truly Rocks!

STORMS AND SNOW, SKIS AND SOX!

New England's Weather Truly Rocks!

Meteorologist
ASHLEY BAYLOR

Globe
Pequot

Essex, Connecticut

Globe
Pequot

An imprint of Globe Pequot, the trade division of
The Rowman & Littlefield Publishing Group, Inc.
4501 Forbes Blvd., Ste. 200
Lanham, MD 20706
www.rowman.com

Distributed by NATIONAL BOOK NETWORK

Copyright © 2022 by Ashley Baylor
Interior design by Amanda Wilson
Map by The Rowman & Littlefield Publishing Group, Inc.

All illustrations © eliflamra/iStock/Getty Images Plus except:
p. 8 hockey skates © AlexBannykh/iStock/Getty Images Plus; p. 11 baseball © Denis08131/
iStock/Getty Images Plus; p. 11 and p. 16 baseball bat, p. 17 baseball glove, p. 25 football
© Bigmouse108/iStock/Getty Images Plus (baseball glove also on the cover); p. 12
shamrock © Dmytro Lukyanets/iStock/Getty Images Plus; p. 13 pot of gold © RoJDesign/
iStock/Getty Images Plus; p. 20 lobster © Irina Griskova/iStock/Getty Images Plus (also on
the cover); p. 21 and p. 31 fireworks © drogatnev/iStock/Getty Images Plus; p. 28 bunting
© filo/DigitalVision Vectors/iStock/Getty Images Plus; p. 28 squash and p. 29 pumpkin pie
and turkey © lattesmile/iStock/Getty Images Plus; p. 32 author photo by Lisa Palmieri

British Library Cataloguing in Publication Information available

Library of Congress Cataloging-in-Publication Data available

ISBN 978-1-4930-5301-8 (paperback)
ISBN 978-1-4930-5302-5 (epub)

Printed in New Delhi, India
March 2022

To my amazing husband, Adam—
Thank you for following me all over the East Coast while I chase my dream. Your love and support mean everything!

To my daughter, Morgan—
You're my sunshine mixed with a little hurricane.
You make life better and brighter!

To my parents—
Thank you for encouraging me, even when things got a little tough.
My #1 fans always!

To my closest friends—
Your positivity inspires me every day.
No matter the distance, I can count on you to always be there and make life a little more exciting!

To all kids who read this book—
The weather is amazing, so keep an eye to the sky!

"Wherever you go, no matter what the weather, always bring your own sunshine."
—ANTHONY J. D'ANGELO

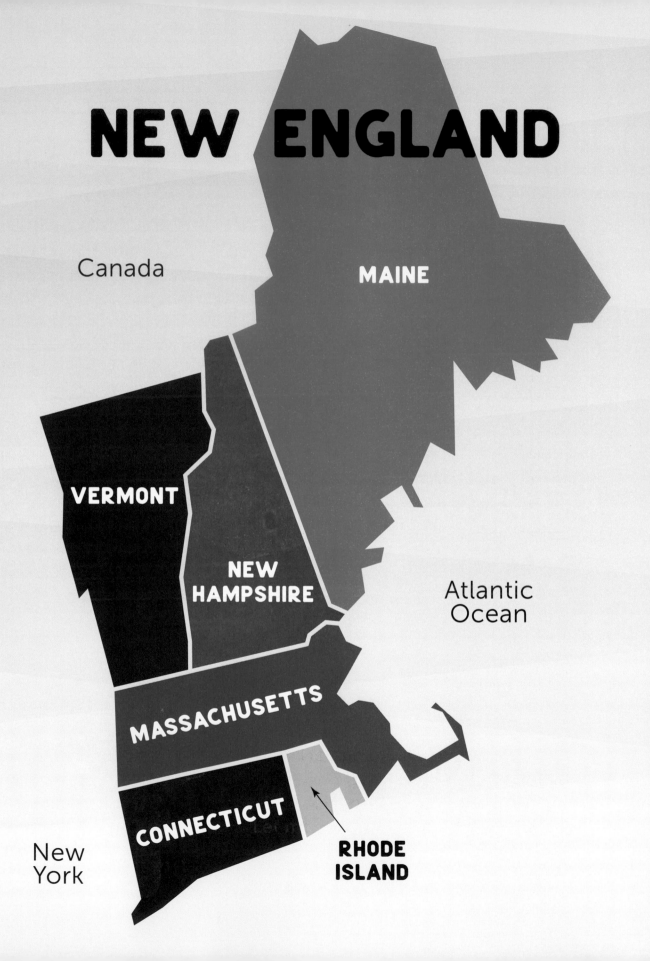

NEW ENGLAND

Canada

MAINE

VERMONT

NEW HAMPSHIRE

Atlantic Ocean

MASSACHUSETTS

New York

CONNECTICUT

RHODE ISLAND

Welcome my friends, thanks for checking this out.
Let's go on an epic journey,
I'll show you what life in New England is all about.

It's a new year, and I have a lot to look forward to.
From aquariums to whale watches,
I'll be exhausted when I'm through.

Maybe I'm a lot like you . . .
I enjoy football, skiing, swimming,
and frequent trips to the zoo.

I live with my mom and dad, and a few rescues.
Our cute pup is Bodie,
the cats are Chase and Bru.

My mom is pretty cool, she's a meteorologist.
So naturally, we love all types of weather . . .
Hail . . . hurricanes . . . too many to list!

I'm turning ten this year, and in fourth grade.
My best buds are Jack and Lucy,
we've been friends for close to a decade.

Hi! How are you? My name is Teddy.
I'm going to take you through a year of my life.
Are you ready?

JANUARY

Watching the news today,
I heard the meteorologist say,
schools may be closed tomorrow because
there's a big nor'easter heading our way!

He said this storm could dump
10 inches or more.
Fresh powder at Sugarloaf?
Let me grab my skis and I'm out the door!

With temperatures only in the teens, that's
some wicked cold air.
I'll pack my warm coat, hat, and gloves . . .
and maybe some long underwear.

It'll be my first time out this season, and I
want to enjoy the day.
Forget Jagger or Ripsaw,
think I'll ski down the new Winter's Way.

FUN FACTS

- A nor'easter is a coastal storm that affects New England and the Mid-Atlantic states.

- The name nor'easter comes from the northeast winds that blow in from the Atlantic Ocean.

- These storms can produce a lot of snow, strong winds, and coastal flooding.

FEBRUARY

Storm after storm,
we have several inches on the ground.
The pile near my house
is just a MASSIVE mound!

Winter break is coming, and I just can't wait!
We are heading to Orlando
and Fort Myers in the Sunshine State!

Flying to Florida, where New Englanders swarm.
We are over the cold,
time to go where it's warm.

With highs in the 70s
and bright sunshine,
theme parks will be packed,
I'll spend my day waiting in line.

From one park to another,
we have tickets to Spring Training.
The Mets will be playing the WET Sox,
since I heard it'll be raining.

FUN FACTS

- Boston averages almost 24 inches of snow between January and February.

- One of the most memorable storms, the Blizzard of '78, happened February 5–7, 1978. Thousands of people were caught in this storm and did not make it home for days. About 3,500 cars were found buried and abandoned on highways during the cleanup.

- On February 8–9, 2013, a nor'easter dumped historic amounts of snow across New England: 40 inches in Hamden, Connecticut; 31.9 inches in Portland, Maine; 28 inches in Worcester, Massachusetts; and 24 inches in Concord, New Hampshire.

MARCH

Going to a Bruins game tonight, they're
on a seven-game winning streak.
My mom surprised me with tickets,
she knows I've had a rough week.

Tomorrow, we are heading to Southie
for the St. Patrick's Day parade.
The forecast says it'll be dry,
so it won't be delayed.

Whether it's warm or cold, sunny or gray—
you will find me decked out in green
and waving on West Broadway.

The weather in March is MADNESS,
which you can't predict with ease.
On Monday it was 70°F,
then Tuesday, it dropped forty degrees!

FUN FACTS

- Cold fronts can cause the temperature to drop quickly—sometimes several degrees within minutes!

- Speaking of temperatures, freezing nights and warm days are the perfect combination for sugaring season in Vermont! That's when folks tap maple trees to make delicious maple syrup!

- Boston is home to the oldest St. Patrick's Day parade in US history, dating all the way back to 1724!

- In 2015 and 2017, the parade route was shortened due to high snow piles.

APRIL

If April showers bring May flowers,
then our backyard will look like a rainforest,
it's been pouring for hours!

It's a good day to watch the Celtics,
who are, *sigh*, ten points behind.
Oh sweet, they're sending in Jayson Tatum,
thank goodness he was signed.

I really want to go outside,
but the wet weather won't quit.
The weatherman said we are going to get two more inches—
I might literally throw a fit.

Run

Tomorrow is Marathon Monday,
so the rain needs to stop.
The runners need cool, dry weather,
and not a single raindrop!

FUN FACTS

- April is an interesting month. New England can get hot days, cold days, rain, snow, and wind.

- The weather for the annual Boston Marathon varies from year to year. In 2015, 2018, and 2019, runners had to deal with driving wind and rain. Runners were shivering as they crossed the finish line! In 2012, it was too warm for runners with temperatures in the high 80s! And yes, the runners have even had to run in the snow!

MAY

It's finally starting to warm up,
so I'm wearing shorts and my new Sox gear.
So long heavy winter coat,
I'll see you next year!

Tonight, under the Green Monstah,
the Sox take on the Yanks.
I'll be singing "Sweet Caroline"
and downing five Fenway Franks.

It's been wicked breezy,
sitting in the grandstand.
Although the wind helped carry a foul ball
right into my hand.

Those New Yorkers will lose—
no doubt!
One . . . two . . . three,
HA! Aaron Judge struck out!

FUN FACTS

- Based on where Fenway Park is located, a southerly or westerly breeze would give the Red Sox the best chance for a home run!

- May can be a wild weather month! On May 15, 2018, four tornadoes touched down in Connecticut, and 100 mph winds blew through Sleeping Giant State Park in Hamden. There was so much damage, the popular park was closed for over a year.

- Snow in May is rare, but it can happen! On May 9, 1977, a late snowstorm dumped 1–2 feet of snow in central Massachusetts and the Litchfield Hills in Connecticut.

JUNE

It's the final month of school,
the last day is three weeks away.
We were supposed to get out earlier,
but we have to make up a few snow days.

I'm looking forward to sleeping in
and long summer days,
but my summer won't be very fun
if I don't get good grades.

I'm doing well in math and science but
struggling in history.
How someone can remember all those
names and dates is a real mystery.

It's hard to study inside when the weather is warm.
Maybe a break in the sunshine will help me brainstorm.

FUN FACTS

- In addition to snow, other forms of severe weather can impact school. On June 1, 2011, three tornadoes tore across western Massachusetts, while two others damaged parts of western and central Maine.

- One of the most historic tornadoes is the 1953 Worcester tornado. The F4 twister was on the ground for an incredible 90 minutes and traveled 48 miles across central Massachusetts. Baseball-size hail was also reported.

- June 1 is also the start of hurricane season, which runs through November 30.

JULY

Summer is here and I have a few goals:
to try sailing and surfing . . .
and one of those Maine lobster rolls!

It's the week of the Fourth
and we are heading to the Cape.
Looking forward to spending my days at the beach,
waiting for big waves to take shape.

We'll start in Chatham
with a tour of the cranberry bog,
then drive down to Lighthouse Beach,
to hear the harbor seals
through the fog.

The parade is on Tuesday,
but skies will be gray.
Hoping the clouds clear out in time
for the annual fireworks display.

FUN FACTS

- Fog is made up of water droplets hovering near the ground.

- Marine fog forms when warmer air moves over the cool ocean water. You can often hear the harbor seals through the fog even though you can't see them.

- Maine is known for their lobsters! The cold Maine water allows lobsters to grow more slowly, which makes for tender and tasty meat!

AUGUST

It's been hazy, hot, and humid
for the past several days.
Afternoon thunderstorms are being fueled
by the sun's rays.

Some storms have been strong,
but most have been weak.
I can't get enough thunder and lightning . . .
I'm turning into a real weather geek.

My mom would be proud,
because she's the *real*
weather nerd . . .
She's tracked blizzards
and tornadoes,
and stood outside in a
hurricane, I heard.

Too bad they don't teach weather in fifth grade,
which I'm starting soon.
This year, I'll be studying rocks and sediments,
instead of cloud types and typhoons.

One way to beat the heat is to stay inside.
It's nice and cool at the aquariums,
you can watch sea lions jump and slide!

FUN FACTS

- ALL thunderstorms produce thunder and lightning, but stronger storms are considered "severe."

- A severe storm can produce a tornado, 58+ mph winds, OR quarter-size hail.

- Mount Washington, New Hampshire, holds the record for fastest *surface* wind speed—231 mph was recorded in 1934!

- Hurricane Bob is a memorable storm for New Englanders. On August 19, 1991, Hurricane Bob made landfall near Newport, Rhode Island, as a Category 2 storm with winds around 100 mph.

SEPTEMBER

Summer was a blast,
now it's Labor Day weekend.
School starts on Tuesday,
and I can't wait to see my friends!

The weather starts to get a little crazy,
similar to June,
freezing with a jacket at seven,
then sweating by noon.

Soon it'll be fall,
my absolute favorite season.
Football, family, and friends,
I don't really need another reason.

Speaking of football,
the regular season just started.
I hope we play the Seahawks and Falcons,
two teams Belichick has outsmarted.

Next week, me and the fam
are heading to the Big E in western Mass,
to stuff ourselves full of
cream puffs and baked potatoes,
followed by a triple bypass.

FUN FACTS

- In September, mornings often start in the 50s, then warm into the 60s and 70s during the afternoon.

- When the air is dry, it warms up quickly—in turn, it also cools down quickly.

- The second week of September is the peak of hurricane season. Hurricane Gloria, another memorable New England hurricane, made landfall near Westport, Connecticut, as a Category 1 storm on September 27, 1985.

OCTOBER

September and October have been busy—
I'm talking weatherwise.
One hurricane after another,
all of them massive in size.

From Harvey, to Irma, to Maria, and Nate,
I was glued to the coverage,
and every Hurricane Center update.

Weeks into October,
you know what that means—
the leaves will be changing color,
turning New England
into a picturesque scene.

Speaking of which,
another place turns into a scene.
Try getting anywhere near Salem
in the weeks leading to Halloween.

Halloween will be here soon,
and I pray there's no snow.
Hey, it's happened before,
just ask Jim Cantore or Paul Goodloe.

FUN FACTS

- In October of 2012, Hurricane Sandy, also known as "Superstorm Sandy," caused significant damage across the northeast. Less than two weeks later, a nor'easter dumped several inches of snow in the same areas affected by Sandy.

- In 2011, an unusually early nor'easter cancelled Halloween activities across southern New England.

- Hey, Patriots fans! The Pats have played in the snow many times, but one of the most memorable games was October 18, 2009. The Pats shut out the Titans 59-0 with snow on the field.

NOVEMBER

GAME DAY

I'll be in Foxborough this Sunday for a big game at Gillette.
The Pats will take on the Falcons—
remember 3–28?
WE won't soon forget!

We are Patriots Nation with the six rings.
But we said so long to Brady, Gronk, and Edelman,
and trust me—it still stings.

My birthday is coming up
and I'm turning the big ONE-OH!
I don't want an iPad or an iPhone,
just new skis and a week at Okemo.

But shortly after my birthday,
there's another day we like to celebrate.
It involves turkey, potatoes, and stuffing!
I've been known to fill a few plates!

Thanksgiving is the absolute best holiday.
While we eat, my mom looks for deals,
prepping for Black Friday.

While she's standing in line,
under a full, cold moon,
I'll be warm in my bed,
and sleeping 'til noon.

FUN FACTS

- One of the most popular Thanksgiving Day events is the Manchester Road Race in Manchester, Connecticut. But the weather isn't always great—in 2018, the wind chill was near zero for the race. In 2005, it snowed!

- November is a great month for football! One of the most popular college games is the annual Harvard-Yale rivalry. "THE GAME" has been played in the rain and snow! Strong winds have also messed up a few field goals!

- Hurricane season ends November 30th. The year 2020 was very active for tropical storms and hurricanes—there were thirty named storms, including seven *major* hurricanes, meaning winds were over 111 mph!

DECEMBER

Back in school,
just for three short weeks.
Christmas vacation is coming,
and I have plans for
Jiminy and Killington Peaks.

Between now and then,
I'm hoping for a lot of snow.
I want Mother Nature
to put on a show!

What's Christmas in New England without a foot . . . or three?
Everyone wants to see the white stuff
while rockin' around the Christmas tree!

We'll welcome the new year soon,
this one has been great.
I hope you've had fun reading,
while I narrate.

There's no place like New England,
I love all the seasons.
Whether it's spring or summer . . . winter or fall,
it's the best place to live for a million reasons!

FUN FACTS

- In December, you may hear people talking about a "white Christmas." A "white Christmas" means at least 1 inch of snow on the ground on Christmas Day.

- Christmas Day 2020 was warm and wet with rain and temperatures in the 60s! On Christmas morning, it was warmer in Burlington, Vermont, than it was in Key West, Florida!

ABOUT THE AUTHOR

Ashley Baylor is a meteorologist for WTNH News 8 in New Haven, Connecticut. Ashley developed a love for weather when she was very young. While living in Charleston, South Carolina, she was glued to the coverage of Hurricane Andrew as it hit southern Florida in 1992. It kickstarted her love of weather, specifically tropical activity. She is a central Massachusetts native, but her career has taken her all over the country, where she has experienced all different types of weather: hurricanes, nor'easters, blizzards, tornadoes, and derechos! Before coming to Connecticut, Ashley worked for WAVY News 10 in Hampton Roads, Virginia; WWLP 22 News in Springfield, Massachusetts; and WEAU 13 News in Eau Claire, Wisconsin. She is a member of the National Weather Association and graduated from the State University of New York at Albany with a degree in broadcast meteorology. She and her husband are HUGE Patriots fans—they married in front of Gillette Stadium in Foxborough, Massachusetts. They are proud parents of their daughter, Morgan; a rescue pup, Bodie; and two Siamese cats, Bruin and Brooklyn.